Written and photographed by
Wayne Lynch

Whose TEETH Are These?

WALRUS
BOOKS

Edited by Elizabeth McLean
Interior design by Warren Clark
Cover design by Peter Cocking
Cover photograph by Wayne Lynch

Printed and bound in Canada

National Library of Canada Cataloguing in Publication Data

Lynch, Wayne.
    Whose teeth are these?

    Includes index
    ISBN 978-1-55285-204-0

    1. Teeth—Juvenile literature I. Title.
QL858.L96 2001   j573.3'56   C2001-910979-2

The publisher acknowledges the financial support of the Canada Council for the Arts, the British Columbia Arts Council, and the Government of Canada through the Canada Book Fund (CBF). Whitecap Books also acknowledges the financial support of the Province of British Columbia through the Book Publishing Tax Credit.

 BRITISH COLUMBIA ARTS COUNCIL

 Canada Council for the Arts   Conseil des Arts du Canada

Can you count how many teeth you have? As a child, you have a tooth for every one of your fingers and toes.

Mostly, you use your teeth to bite and chew your food. But you also use your teeth when you smile, and this tells people you are friendly.

Many wild animals have teeth that look very different from yours. Some of their teeth are pointed like needles, some are as big as a baseball bat, and some are brightly colored. See if you can figure out who owns the teeth in this book.

Even when I grow up, I have no front teeth on my upper jaw. When I eat grass, I use my tough gum and lower teeth to break it off. In winter when the snow is deep, I eat mostly twigs and bark. With my long neck and long legs, I can reach bark high up on the trunk of a tree. I use my lower teeth like a file to scrape off the tasty bark.

Who am I?

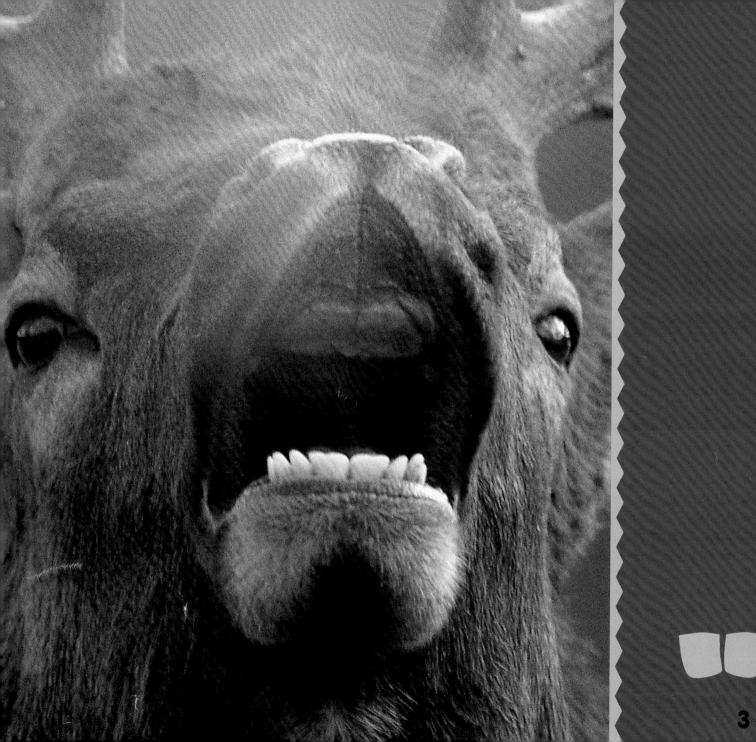

I am a bull elk, and I belong to the deer family, which also includes moose and caribou. I live in the forests of North America, Europe, and Asia.

Every year, I grow a new pair of bony antlers on my head, like branches on a tree. I use my large antlers to wrestle with other bull elk and to impress female elk.

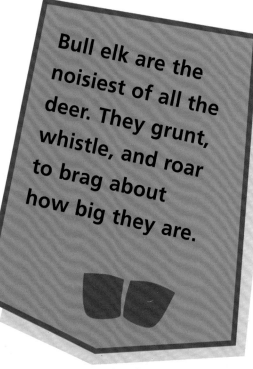
Bull elk are the noisiest of all the deer. They grunt, whistle, and roar to brag about how big they are.

I have very strange teeth. I use the bumps on my teeth to scrape off small plants that grow on rocks in the ocean. Juicy plants are my favorite food, and sometimes I dive deep underwater to reach them. When I stay in the water too long, my body gets cold and stiff. Then I lie in the hot sun to warm up.

Who am I?

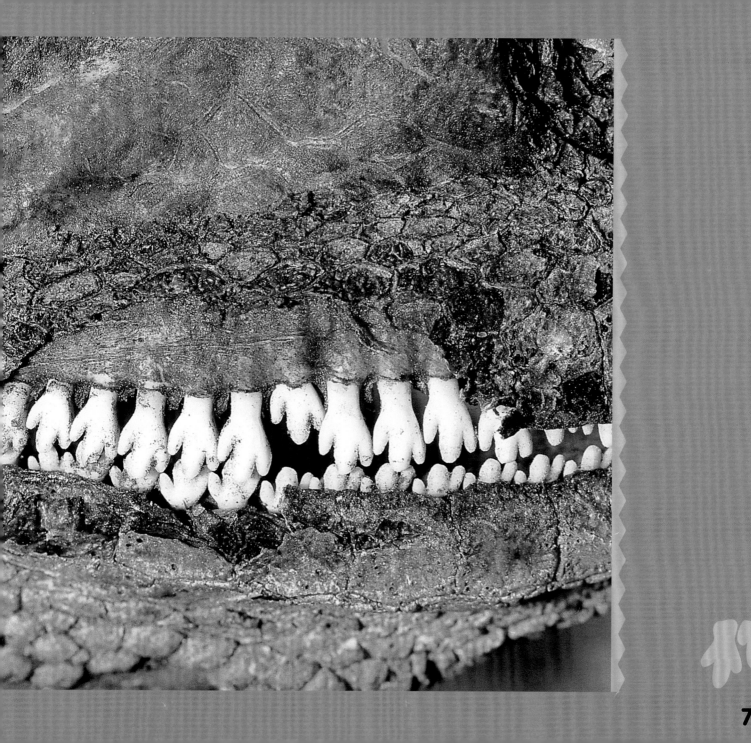

I am a marine iguana, the only lizard that gets its food from the ocean. My home is in the Galapagos Islands, where many unusual animals live.

I have a long, flat tail to help me swim, and sharp claws to grip the slippery rocks. When I eat, I sometimes swallow salty water. To get rid of the salt, I sneeze it out of my nose.

I use the pointed scales on my head to butt other iguanas and push them around.

9

The orange coating on the front of my teeth is very hard, so my teeth are always sharp. That's important, because I use my teeth to cut down trees. I like to eat the bark and small branches, and I use the bigger branches to make a house in the water. I am an excellent diver, and can swim far underwater.

Who am I?

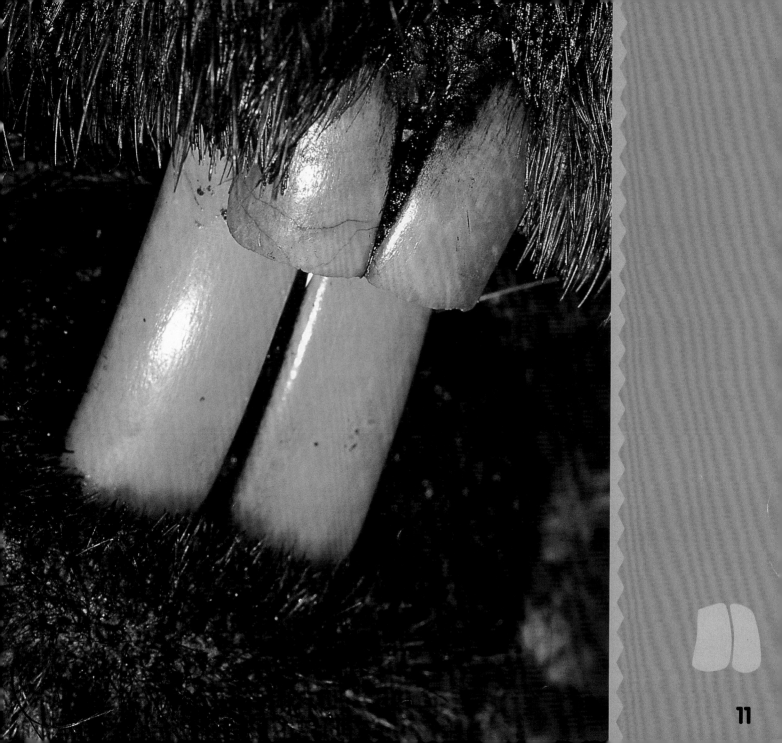

11

I am a beaver, one of the biggest buck-toothed rodents. I live in lakes and ponds throughout North America, and am a great builder.

Before I build a house, I often make a log dam to raise the water in the pond where my family lives. Deep water keeps us safe from hungry wolves, bears, and cougars. Sometimes, nine or ten of us squeeze inside the same house.

When there is danger, I slap the water with my flat tail. It makes a loud noise to warn other beavers.

ow, what a big mouth I have! I use my sharp front teeth to scare my neighbors away, because I like to be alone. I am a scavenger, so I mostly eat animals that are already dead. The large teeth at the back of my mouth are useful to crush bones and cut through tough skin.

Who am I?

Maybe you guessed I was a hyena, but I am a Tasmanian devil, and I live in Australia. During the day, I hide in a hollow tree or cave, and only come out when it is dark.

When I find a dead kangaroo, I try to chase other devils away. But a hungry devil is hard to scare, so many of us may eat together. Mealtime is noisy because we hiss, growl, and scream when we eat.

A female devil has a pouch for her young, like a kangaroo. The pouch opens backwards, so dirt doesn't get in when she digs.

My front teeth are like hollow needles that I use to inject deadly venom. The venom kills the mice, voles, and ground squirrels that I hunt. Once the animals are dead, I swallow them whole. Many small, sharp teeth inside my mouth help me to do this. I can even swallow animals that are bigger than my head.

Who am I?

I am a diamondback rattlesnake. I live in the prairies and deserts of North America. The diamond pattern on the scales of my back gives me my name.

I use my forked tongue to taste the air for danger. When I am frightened, I shake the rattle on the end of my tail to scare away enemies.

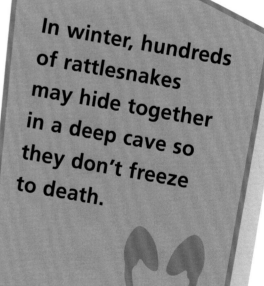

In winter, hundreds of rattlesnakes may hide together in a deep cave so they don't freeze to death.

My front teeth can grow as big as a baseball bat, and I might use them to help me walk. That's why my nickname is toothwalker. I can also use my long teeth like a sledgehammer, to chop holes in the ice when the ocean freezes. My big teeth are called tusks. They are handy to jab my buddies when they crowd me on a beach.

Who am I?

I am a walrus, and I can weigh more than a small car. I get so fat by eating buckets and buckets of clams, sea cucumbers, and worms every day.

My whiskers are useful to feel for food on the bottom of the Arctic Ocean. When I find a juicy clam, I suck it up like a vacuum cleaner, and leave the shell behind.

Only a polar bear or a killer whale is big and strong enough to attack a full-grown walrus.

I am a fierce hunter. I use my front teeth like daggers to attack moose, elk, and deer. I sneak as close as I can, then leap on my prey and bite the back of its neck. When I kill a big animal, I can't eat it all at once. I cover it with grass and dirt to hide it from ravens. Then I can come back later for another meal.

Who am I?

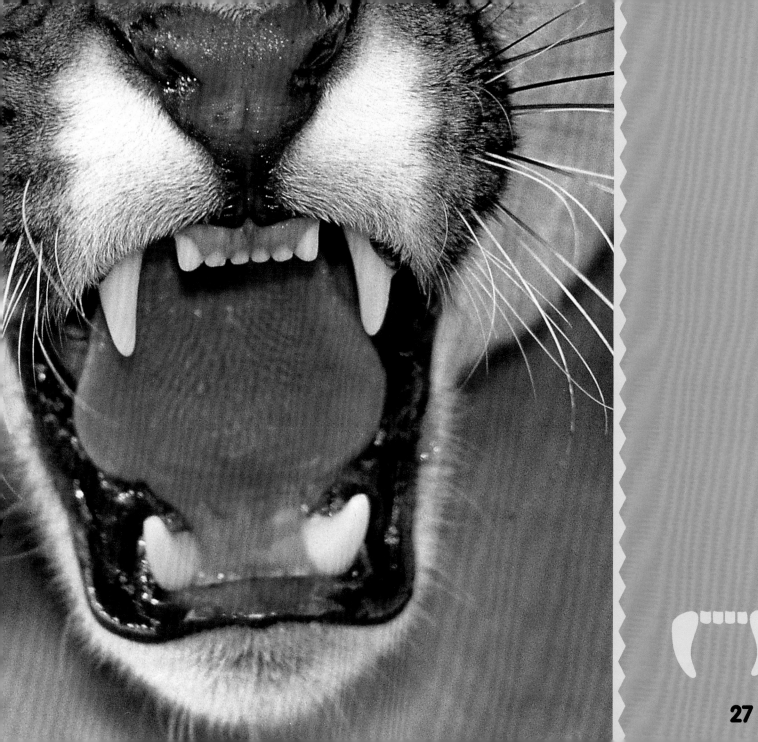

I am a cougar, the largest cat in North America. Some people call me a mountain lion or puma. I live in the western mountains, and in the swamps of Florida.

A male cougar will scratch tree trunks and rake the ground with his claws, just like a housecat. This sends a message to other male cougars to stay away.

A female cougar can have up to six kittens in a litter. They may stay with her for two years while they learn to hunt.

Index

570.3